absentia

Also by William Stobb

Nervous Systems

PENGUIN POETS

William Stobb

~

absentia

PENGUIN BOOKS

Published by the Penguin Group
Penguin Group (USA) Inc., 375 Hudson Street, New York, New York 10014, U.S.A.
Penguin Group (Canada), 90 Eglinton Avenue East, Suite 700, Toronto, Ontario,
Canada M4P 2Y3 (a division of Pearson Penguin Canada Inc.)
Penguin Books Ltd, 80 Strand, London WC2R 0RL, England
Penguin Ireland, 25 St Stephen's Green, Dublin 2, Ireland (a division of Penguin Books Ltd)
Penguin Group (Australia), 250 Camberwell Road, Camberwell, Victoria 3124, Australia
(a division of Pearson Australia Group Pty Ltd)
Penguin Books India Pvt Ltd, 11 Community Centre, Panchsheel Park, New Delhi - 110 017, India
Penguin Group (NZ), 67 Apollo Drive, Rosedale, Auckland 0632, New Zealand
(a division of Pearson New Zealand Ltd)
Penguin Books (South Africa) (Pty) Ltd, 24 Sturdee Avenue, Rosebank,
Johannesburg 2196, South Africa

Penguin Books Ltd, Registered Offices:
80 Strand, London WC2R 0RL, England

First published in Penguin Books 2011

1 3 5 7 9 10 8 6 4 2

Copyright © William Stobb, 2011
All rights reserved

Page xi constitutes an extension of this copyright page.

CIP data available
ISBN 978-0-14-312018-6

Printed in the United States of America

Set in Century Old Style Std
Designed by Ginger Legato

In memoriam

Jay Meek, Earl Madary, Chris Whitley
SPC Rachel Hugo, Liam Fannin

Contents

One

~

Two

~

~

~

Acknowledgments

I am grateful to the editors of the following publications, in which many of these poems were first published: *American Poetry Review, Colorado Review, Conduit, DIAGRAM, Jacket, Konundrum Engine Literary Review, MiPOesias, OCHO, Oranges & Sardines, Phoebe, Poetry Flash, The Offending Adam, Southwestern American Literature*, and *Touchstone*.

Some of these poems appeared in a limited-edition chapbook of desert fragments entitled *Artifact Eleven* (Reno: Black Rock Press, 2011).

Some of these poems appeared in a downloadable chapbook for mobile devices entitled *Pointless Channel* (Goss 183, 2010).

Special thanks to David Krump, who read many drafts of many of these poems.

absentia

One

Channels, Currents, Crossings

~

No road in 1960, so they dragged the cabin
across ice, installed it after thaw.
Forty years later, sun- and wind-tired,
four children lounge in front of satellite television.
Four parents, old friends, stand at the windows
of a screened-in porch, trying to gauge
a reasonable level of concern:
against heavy northerlies, four-foot swells,
a motorboat struggles to pull a sailboat
back to harbor. Eight p.m. Boats barely advancing.
The two men hunkered in the hull
—friends? brothers? afraid?

We put the children to bed.
When we come back out, the boats are beyond us.

~

As if looking down at something
shining in deep water, we view our former selves.
The solstice sun pinwheels along the northern shore
and day extends beyond our supply of wine.
Riding persistent wind, the lake grows louder.
Finally overtaken, I try to turn in
but can't find quiet inside, either.
I read by flashlight about a woman
who emptied herself for passages.
"What requires me channels through."

My thoughts return to the two men,
probably drinking at a bar, telling their brave tale
or dreaming through the crest and trough
their bodies are slow to surrender.

~

After three, I drift back to the porch
to see the sun skim the northern rim.
Wind's calmed some
but the agitated lake still hacks at the beach.
This place seems impossible.
The expanse of water, frenzied or frozen,
too great an obstacle.
Thinking toward the furthest reaches of my life
I watch starlight bounce away from the chop—
many precise trajectories
woven above the surface of the lake.

I wonder if I am awake.

Then our youngest cries and late dissolves in early.
The last look I gather's a gray field punctured
by the peak of another first sail out of harbor.

Vanishing Act

What sound there is—whisper of wind
across the land's sand skin—becomes muffled,
lightly punctuated by blood pulse.   Sediment
lines on surrounding foothills indicate gone
water.
                              Stake the imaginary tent
on imaginary lake bottom. Cartoon fish blow
bubbles in the flap.

                    This same day—same
drizzle scrim, same gray gauze drawn down
over everything—ten thousand years ago
in some kind of almanac.

                    No one admits Mother's vague
in memory, in rooms as energy, a scribble cloud
vibrating in a hard chair.   Glacial lake.
Everything shaken out of gray sheets of sky, so
low there's no distinction.

                         No one imagines the boy
lonely.

        Was there a word for one form freezing
in another? And one for trying to breathe
underwater?

        Lightning's broken ladder makes
over there out of former shore. Train crosses

the playa edge, ten miles off.   Meltwater
follows crevice into porous rock. Wind wears
the faces. The ghost town folds. Inside erases.
                              The sky crosses over.

Little Disintegration

Wheeler Peak

To canyon crevasse and sun
wheel spun under a million
visible stars unsuspecting
voyagers are called
to disintegrate and report back.
One used a pocket knife
to saw where his arm was crushed
beneath a boulder—descended delirious
a glacier to camp where
his belongings had already been burned.
Saved he said gradually everything
splinters. A sleepless teenager
I stepped into night wanting
to live soon, here.
I didn't imagine this overstimulated
prone to drinking
near tears drifting toward
sleep beside my five-year-old.
Silver field of his tummy hairs
shimmering in strange
night-light aura—by attending
I would merge and by merging
rebuild civilization in me.
Settlers to this country
pushed rickety carts across
deep time through
their own bodies to geology
beyond West inside.
Desert peak teetered up by cooling
surface stretching to fault and rift.

Ten thousand years
a grove petrifies on the ridgeline.
Polished by elements at some elevation
I grew up. And away.

At the Edge of Perfect Adequacy

Harsh and consoling, deeply roaming
final precincts of oblivion and trials of encounter.

Neither unbounded singularity nor dread
of solitude, best known unmasked,
we emit organized sounds in the shape of X.

There is no complete echo.
There is no free animal.

Three roads meet between Thebes and Delphi.
Conduct springs from wells deeper than
a private tongue refusing any relation.

Inward eye to purchase wider than.
Peregrine toward waking
the persuasion of our fiber.

Our condition is stranger.

The Pinky of Great Sugi

I ended up talking with a young botanist
who seemed a little lost at a bar party.
I'd recently seen the bristlecone pines at Wheeler Peak

and he listened as I described the hike:
the strange entangled trees clinging to granite
and the stump of the dead Prometheus—
once the oldest living organism, cut for research.

He walked away. I worried
I'd bored him. I lingered at the edge of other
conversations. A bit later

he came right to my shoulder.
More visible in the bar back lantern glow
—his face a figure eight between lamb chop sideburns,
eyes set apart and flush on mine, assessing—

he handed me a small envelope
with something like a cylinder inside.
"I couldn't believe what you were saying, before.

I just returned from Japan where I visited
Great Sugi of Kayano—no exaggerated sagebrush,
Sugi's a hundred and sixty feet tall.
And at seven thousand years old,

he's earned the status of a priest.
Commoners and emperors alike approach him
with questions about their lives.

I went to see the old master
but met a protective barrier. Why had I imagined
I would touch him? Thwarted,
I felt the mystery of my journey fading.

Then standing there with my head hung low,
I noticed scattered sprigs that could only have
belonged to Great Sugi. Suddenly revitalized

I picked one for my mother, one for myself,
and one for my partner, here in Vancouver,
who felt very near to me then.
I had not arrived with a question in mind

but after receiving these gifts
I felt eager to take instruction
from the oldest being I had seen, so I asked,

'Great Sugi, how will I ever let go of this living?'
I waited. The wind blew the same. Birds continued
to dip and dart. Tourists posed and smiled.
I offered a bow and walked away.

When I returned home—just three days ago—
my partner was gone. His life with me was wrong.
He left a note. I hadn't even known."

I tapped the envelope into my palm—a twig
like a pinky run with thorns up the bone.
"It's okay," said the botanist. "I want to be alone."
He returned to the dim, busy scene

and I tried to handle
the barbed relic, detached but still
integral, potent, resistant to the touch.

Memorial

in memoriam SPC Rachel Hugo (1983–2007)

A young woman I knew in a subtle way
—a charge in her aggressive questions,
a change in the quality of air, light
in her hair, the expression
of some presence unwarranted
by our contact—served as a medic in Iraq.
When her vehicle came under attack
she went to the aid of a wounded Lieutenant
took fire from what we now call insurgents
and died there, along that roadside.

Away from the dispersing crowd
after her candlelight service
I leaned in shadow near a statue of St. Francis
pinned between sun and moon.
Among mourners scattering under streetlamps,
I tried to regain my sense of her.
What was that connection? What was real?
And though I didn't understand it
the feeling or idea came
that I could release her from that place.
I tried to open myself, believe,
and allow a freedom to happen through me.

Later that night I sat under the ancient
lilac that marks the border
between my shade garden
and the koi pond my neighbor Randy installed.
I drank a beer. It was cold out and clear.
I didn't want to go inside and talk, read, watch TV.

I tried not even thinking, sitting
in a plastic chair, surrendered
to night's common deceptions:
calm air—distant light points
as something other than explosions.

Then a noticing part duly registered
a silhouette crossing Randy's dim patio.
I attended to its shape and motion and thought
what a slow, quiet dog
climbing the downspout.

Not a dog. An opossum.

Careful not to be abrupt, I stood
and stepped to the fence that extends the boundary.
Night-lit silver-tinged creature angled its oval face up to me.
Dark eye circles. Steam ribbons
from its dark nostril circles.
In a long moment of mutual regard,
some recognition opened—I opened
the window and she laughed when the draft
blew through and papers and her hair
went everywhere until
the door slammed shut—
then released and the creature
wobbled into the other kind
of night that was its life.

The Naturalist and the Ant Lion

The naturalist notices a pit in the sand.
He draws his audience closer, scans
the surface, bends, pinches an ant,
drops the ant in the pit, which is a cone
cast at the angle of repose
so, watching, everyone knows
the ant can't escape.
Ant scrambles. Sand shivers.
From the pit base
mandibles emerge.
It's a nightmare for ants,
a crab trap transition that can't be
untriggered except
like magic the naturalist extracts
and separates predator from prey.
The ant bumbles away as we
merely examine the bulbous ant lion
—bloated, glamourless, a moment's demonstration
of intelligence shaping and transferring energy.

Boom

In a system of fault block ranges, distance
as pure concept manifests three long flats.
Roughnecks and engineers gather
to race rocket cars against thunder.

Seems like another planet where anyone would care.

We went there as friends to see
what being friends would be like
on Mars. It was awesome.
Fires near and fires far. One or two
words against sediment and stars.

Then they rolled out the rocket car.

We traced carvings—the spiral, the net—
stood in stone husks of shoreline huts
where a fishing village blinked
into geology. A hundred years or fifteen
thousand. All past inhabited.

They rolled out the rocket car.

Long black engine with a tiny space for a person.
Like an insect out of black water
it emerged from its own heat haze,
burned a fire line across the playa.

Something changed—the air cracked open

and wobbled into a hobbled kind of boom
—but we understood change in all things.
We weren't confused.

We stayed and watched the race team vanish.

Absentia

"Did I tell you? I think I did.
I liked your speech at the conference.
Kind of a walk-by on the steps outside:
'hey I liked your speech now we're astronauts
drifting apart through deep space—
I liked your speeeeeeeech.'
It reminded me of feelings
I had when M.'s baby died.
Those big eyes, *remember?*
They wash through my mind.
Long lashes long absence.
A whole life can you imagine
of absence? The Laotian boy in your speech.
Did he really run away
to fight in the secret army
then meet his mother at Safeway in Sheboygan?
It made me breathe in that sobby way.
I had a hard time sitting quietly.
Hearing you. Seeing you on a stage.
I couldn't make myself stay.

Can we try again in the spring?
I hope you're feeling the world
appreciates you adequately.
I appreciate you so much
I can't see you. Isn't it funny
saying 'the world' all the time like we know?
Mostly I know things that can't quite
seem to happen."

Dictionary No Dictionary

"The world is all that is the case."

—Ludwig Wittgenstein

(why I write these definitions
for shit I don't even have a handle on like
"exchange of swirly shapes
through inner and outer space"—a butterfly
in Madison blows out a harmonica
in Portland and this is the world
okay? This is the place, Johnson
to Boswell, "the taste," to Tate,
"the oblivion") ha ha. In mine
Mother had a knee replaced
then fell and popped her shoulder
("world"). Better than my uncle
who had to grow new muscles
to swallow pills meant almost to
kill him. "More than that summer
week at your cabin" and love
can unravel you remember:
some debris makes burning arcs across the sky.
From mine subtract fifteen orbits of friendship
like old-school surgery I'm unconscious
flayed gently beeping then punching
numbers and somewhere a cell
rings. You answer. Our lives are
not saved. Mainly
I wonder what else happened?
What's your ring tone?
What did the waiter think of you crying then snap
to the cook who slaps what on the omelet
(rings bell—"Nine's up!")

meant for you but served to the Senator?
"Pull hard on those handcuffs."
Something I've not heard during sex play
but does that disqualify it metaphysically?
Pull the chain. "Like a dog," Josef K.
Face the honest explanation
of ten years in your parents' basement.
See the links attached to this
paying of attention ("The sum
of all facts, fronts, flags for facing")? Pull.
A Russian soldier on Nevsky Prospekt
opened beer bottles with his arm stubs.
For souvenirs I bought posters
for communism ("explosions
on every level to scale beyond
thinking"). I'm anti-
place you say in a paper ("Where anyone
can sit quietly and ring a chime"). No
to faces. No to cases. Rapidly blinking
the world erases. One white beam
pixels your iris. A simple yes
and we're through.

I Try to Think

> "A thing there was that mattered."
>
> —Virginia Woolf

Packed sand, branches, nettles, shoreline.
But then airport, port-o-potty, sanitized
cubicle where coverage expires.
One surprise at the Moscow station:
humans crumpled in fluorescent sleep. Afraid
at customs I'd never understand
sent to Siberia but she stopped yelling
let me through to Fish Fabrique
where one old Russian hippie kept his
John Lennon peace and love shrine.
There. Then. What could I have been thinking?
A question I've asked when memory heaves
back another city's abutments.
Most of the time nuclear war.
From '83 when the Reds dropped Jason
Robards with that fake Kansas blast
until oh two when the nuclear
part was just the tip to bust the bunker
which I always thought of as a golf
not a gulf word. I dreamed
Osama's mountain lair—
lighted tennis courts under granite tonnage
his high toss under high voltage
perfect C-pose serve in white robes.
I took another viewing of *Beneath
the Planet of the Apes*. Obsessive traits
run in families. After a fight
but before major security
we went to the airport, watched jets

leap the ravine into cumulus
clouds with sculptural properties—
I thought of invisible pressures
roughing up cabins-full of married people.
I wondered how they taught Sunday school
in those basement rooms
knowing wildness in every moment's
eighty-six religions. For a while
deserts only seemed good for war. Then I lived
in one and found it good for Frisbee.
For a while it seemed
I'd never share a sensible word with my father.
Then he said he might've murdered the whole committee
if they'd sent him back to China.
Ruins compressed in geological strata.
Intersection of county roads
after consecutive untended millennia.
A squirrel got trapped in my friend's parents' cabin
and died trying to chew through a window frame.
Glacial runoff's pristine, refreshing.
Lit by a rig in flames on the surface
a child's sparkly sandal drifting down.

Release

not a phase   too much thinking
broke me   dog next door out for a pee
someone's little laugh
worms in wood   old words splinter
winter into spring   popular piano music
and a warm front from Alberta

under the brewery towers
the formerly broken
marquee sparkles   that open flame
in the industrial park   so not eternal
has a name
                    release
sound of the day   ice dam
explodes the river into flow

Emergent

All the time the dual working of my mind
distracted me.

Features surface through long
hair, white-lit in fluorescent wattage. Watching
myself inside. Narrow channel between bay and
body of my childhood lake.   Mountain
named after a prostitute but I prefer thinking of
her physical face upturned.

The hopeless dream
of being (her whole range, languid in relation to
sky). To escape complicated family, I stare at
the shore, emerge there, cross the narrow strand
and plunge into opposite forest.

Living
kind of pivots around. All fluid realism. Blue
idea behind rock, the lake narrows to where I
stand, waiting for fish to appear in my hands.

Written While Filling the Kiddie Pool

So that my children when they arrive
will have warm water to splash in.
Hose over lip. Water drum plastic.

"Lives of the Vice Presidents," I begin,
drawn to some glimmer in their distant names—
Fillmore, Van Buren, Schuyler Colfax and Chester Arthur.

Maybe ten minutes while it's filling:
Presidents face the challenges of their office
while the Vices nearly govern, pen

memos, forget capitals, blunder
into pistol duels in misty forests.
The afternoon sun warms shallow water

as a Vice President nods off in a vestibule
and I too recline beside a young maple.
The turtle-shaped pool nearly full

the Vice Poem settles for second.
Oh well, no big poem.
It was really nothing, goes the song,

but then *it was your life*, it goes
and that's kind of a bummer—
sitting in a smallish circle of shade

in a larger circle of failed ideas.
That children will arrive or are arriving.
That arriving's begun and I only have to wait.

Classic mistake.
Planting this sapling I confronted
many wrong ideas about the ground:

Hades, MoleMan, China down there and China Syndrome.
One thing's true: you can't just dig for fear
of puncturing the mythical and actual fabric

of buried wire you could call Persephone's
Panties. Or not. But you do
call a hotline and the next day flags appear.

The future arrives—all clear for digging—as current
might overwhelm a body, children shatter
the latch, pour through the garden gate.

Aaron Burr's bullet unwinds Hamilton's alternate
future—squiggly lines buzz up the arms—
hair straightens, ears smoke—children pause

midair as if thinking made plastic
swimming pools, maple trees, time
stills as water equals its container

then exceeds
and spills
into now.

Natural History

Canceled by virtue of its own best qualities
the desert produced its idea. A pleasured region arches its back, a canyon
bursts, and five hundred valleys fill like kiddie pools.

Or are we
just having a bad weekend here? Everything's a joke?

I wanted a machinelike
transaction. I wanted to make direct statements and then directly receive
the help those statements purchased. But in warm interactions more
emotions come through. If nothing strikes you as off-kilter, a person
might be honest.

I think of it as this place that became exactly
what it wanted to be, like a very confident child.

Who shot Lassen?
No one knew, so an Indian was invented—magical rider, rifleman,
dancing out of sight along the ridgetops.

It felt simple and good
to talk about sex, but dangerous, too, like swimmers happily splashing
before sharks bite them in half.

I'm in here writing this and you're out
there laughing still.

Spiral and net
carved in tufa along lakeshore benchmarks caterpillared by sage. Photos
of Clark Gable's trophy trout in the Paiute interpretive center. "He could
sure play a broken-down wrangler."

"Then I get to make a rule," I
began. If she could say "I'm coming with you and you can't stop me,"
then I could say something absolute. But she didn't know what I meant,
and I didn't know what rule to make anyway.

Artifact of no
known purpose: star ritual, self-sifter, myth sister. Who knows

what's going on in another person's head? Like one hotel tower standing
next to another one. People playing slots, watching pay-per-view, trying
to get laid or get something to happen anyway for real and quick. The
present has to make the future worthy.

Elephant carving on a high boulder.
Sheep. Shaman. Masks. (Remember the gallery of matchstick masks and
safari game on the back wall at Jeannie's?)

The grid a hallucination.

I'm having a good time
but I get tired of listening to loud music and making sex jokes. Alkali
floods, dries and cracks. The breathing underneath. The city they build
and bomb. The man they build and burn.

Otherwise I worry
about our friendship.

I Am in Your Experimental Novel

I don't say thank you when the server
brings a ramekin of cream.

Misty Riverwood is my porn star name.

I have a line: "I was bitten by a shark."
I cannot uncover your narrative arc.

I have love in my life. I have children.
My daughter catches me smoking from a glass pipe.

I wonder: am I the type to shatter
scatter shrapnel across a hundred pages?

I am not your main character but I am mine.

Once in our lives, we should kiss on the lips.
If my hand drifts you replace it in its proper domain.

You and vague boy move to Santa Fe.

As a gesture of consolation, you entrust me
with a houseplant that overgrows my room.

Entangled, pierced and absorbed
I could snap, disappear, or dissolve,

but you make me simple. I ride
by your old house. Have I survived? I'm surprised.

I stop pedaling but glide into bread scent.

Do I always ride to the bakery this early?
From somewhere, this arrives, unfounded, this feeling

of hope that seems quite convenient for you.

Cloud Out of Square

From the top of the city bakery
pours an enormous cloud of steam

even when it's warm out and calm
up through industrial oven hoods
circular cluster of hook-shaped vents
a metal bow streaming ribbon on a stucco gift

but today at windchill minus fifteen
heat and bread scent billow
panic white inside out into blue
flatten over Cass Street to rapidly cool

curl on a downdraft the old hotel
splash on pavement and rush
across the intersection
all around me

Blue in Nature and Some Overflow

in memoriam Earl Madary (1965–2006)

A year later I ride through the marsh.
A goose hisses at me.
A heron flees the racket my bike trailer makes.

I hadn't even thought of you yet.
I had to run Hawaiian Punch
to my daughter's school

and grocery shop for Anna's graduation.
I had to try once or twice
to stay positive. When Claire called to tell me

we forgot the luau I didn't get angry.
Maybe one second.
A dog came bounding

over hillocks of marsh grass growing
around root-balls and trunks decomposing.
It wasn't scary. Some kind of hound

probably practicing birding
only these birds weren't shot. I thought
of you only after the trail submerged

—luckily my trailer has good clearance
but my shoes got soaked. (Would you have
thought to put your shoes in the trailer? I didn't.)

Only after that bracing adventure
did I cross the bridge, look down
at the overflown oxbow

and remember you
securing your canoe to get up on a gnarly deadfall
and help Andy and me clear a gap that wasn't

nearly as narrow as we were making it seem.
You came back to me clearly—
feeling really good you said meds were effective—

when one of those little birds you see
a million of but also only individual ones rarely—
glimpses of the bird world much more

than hi how do you do singular bird
I know you now
we're fine acquaintances and friends for life—

jigged away from whatever
it was snacking up right off the pavement—
I was riding easy no rush just busy

in my head with you feeling *good* so relatively
close in time to my talking
to your corpse on the sofa in the side room

and it jigged up and away from my approach
then in a pretty tight moment
snapped back to take one more bite I guess

it was really good and it knew
it had plenty of time I was happy to see
as I remembered you

the bird posed for
the briefest interlude vividly blue.

Some Overflow

This thinking overflows the poem. About how musical it was—the zigzag the bird made in its deft fly-away-and-then-back and its clear, momentary pose all made me think of how like instruments we are played by perception and consciousness. I turned the bike and trailer around, rode back and found the bird again. It had an ample source of food in seeds fallen on the trail—we're right in the middle of a late spring bloom—so I was sure I'd find it again and I did. And when I managed to get close enough to see it clearly a second time, I thought and felt that the bird was only itself now. In that first moment when its performance blew through me it had been more. Not, "it had signified more," though I know it's absurd to argue that I didn't interpret it. It was more than itself. It was bright arpeggios separated by an eighth note rest. It was you, Earl. But in the second instance, it was itself only. "Of course it has its own life," I thought. These thoughts about *how* the dead are with us—the mechanism of it, though that sounds awful. Maybe the instrumentation of it—the ways we're blown through the larger harmonic. Maybe the dead play the symphony of the living, though after I wrote "At the Afterlife Hotel" I started really hating metaphors about what the dead are doing. I wanted to think of the dead very physically, strung through the ground and plants and air and blood. And then I think of you and blue appears in nature. Physical blue. Even a blue flower but in this case better, an animate creature, softly textured and coming still as if to present itself as blue in response to the thought, so precious as if dropped from some richer sphere. This thinking overflows as maybe living overflows.

Two

a dream: that there is an ecstasy in life unfolding over billions of years, and therefore no human is ever unnatural or disordered

—Earl Madary

Holiday

"At that time I was kind of living
a monastic life, or that's how I thought of it.
In the morning, I would play a few
notes on the piano, like a chime.
Then I would sit and look out the window.
I didn't think of painting. I tried
not to. I didn't think of the people
I had hurt and left behind.
I saw the world elapsing—
not just changing but unwinding before my eyes.
I could sit perfectly still, impassive,
and feel the peace of mind endings imply.
One fall day a cardinal was appearing
and vanishing and appearing again
on the poplar overhanging the street.
Its motions untied a ribbon
in the mist shrouding the distant bluff top.
All morning it got darker
and I recognized the familiar
sense of things unraveling. The sky
opened and hail began at first tapping
then attacking so violently
I had to admit I was afraid.
Frozen stones shredded the poplar
and I wondered if the cardinal had been
able to find shelter. Quite suddenly
a black van pulled to the curb.
A man emerged and, protecting his head
with a briefcase, dashed up my sidewalk.
Thinking he was in trouble—
fully exposed in a dangerous storm—
I went to let him in. That would be

unnecessary. Before I could reach the door,
which I would've sworn was locked,
he entered my home without permission.
And although he would neither speak
nor ever be identified by any authority
I felt a vivid sense of recognition.
For a moment—before he showed me
things I would do to stay alive—
I felt at ease, as if time had flung back
a holiday memory. The stranger smiled
and I said 'hello.' "

The Sights and Sounds of Morning

Run early get home coffee's automatically made
eat fruit shower dress kiss
wife leaving for work hustle
children through the kitchen and out
to the sidewalk—love you be good
get smart be nice love you love you bye.

Before I start writing this,
water new grass seed planted
where dog piss brought up dirt.
After hose hiss something
walkie-talkie? in the alley
stop listen notice eventually
count six small birds
hunting the interior of our lilac tree.
Mostly some kind of finch or sparrow
but one woodpecker in there I see
ripping bugs out of old wood.
Birds live this way but trees die
so I ring the chime to scare him off
like I can stop the processes.
Lovely pattern doesn't even
look at me—red crown striking striking
in decay I call landscaping.
Again the walkie-talkie
what the hell is going on?
I poke my nose across the fenceline.
Between squad cars behind my garage
two officers in riot gear
flank a neighbor smoking
a cigarette with his two
cuffed hands.

Poem of Sobriety

In the month I quit drinking
I slept a great deal. I worried
sobriety was my prostration unto death.
Drunk, I would never have said that.

So the Cranes of Baraboo
trained to follow an ultralight
migrated with assistance to Florida.
And the pulverized innards of those other fowl
which scrapped an airliner's engines
—those are called snarge.

Death to the psychopathic billionaire scam artist!
African rebel calls a presser
to officially retire from terror.
Displaced soldiers sling AKs and wander.

I would drink again.

The Russian ballerina's shoulders
described as "ravishing," her "sultry" lips and leaps
like afterthoughts—"beyond the dreams
of the common reader."

Poem of Inevitability

It's inevitable that I won't be able
to not drink that wine, I almost said, but didn't.

I went upstairs with Carter
who inevitably opened *The Encyclopedia*

of Spider-Man to the page about Hammerhead.
His skull is flat for knocking over buildings.

Jackal leers in the rafters, and there's Cold Pin,
boss of crime. It's Kingpin. Yeah? Yep.

In an arctic air mass a sense of inevitability
drives boys to ponder the death of Harry Osborn.

Claire mixes Avril Lavigne songs in the hallway
as if reborn. I fall asleep for two hours

and inevitably wake, fully rested, at midnight.
In the event I become my mother

rather than father I'll need rubber gloves.
Hang on I want to add that to my list for tomorrow.

And my dream of Spider-Girl—criminal? sister?
—in the day's echo I'll drift washing dishes

watch moonlight on the frost pack.
I'll be elsewhere and won't hear the bottles

shiver in the wine rack.

Poem on Earth

for Mary Jean Stobb

For half an hour we had that kind of snow
where there's so much moisture in the air
and the air's so cold
that each flake's crystal system
is elaborate lace and surprisingly large.
                    My sympathies
to radiology technicians
working in belowground medical facilities
and dedicated attendants
of presidential escape routes
standing all day at their secret posts
with everything slung on their belts—
pagers, mag lights, nine millimeter issue.
Nothing ever happens
yet their pants are falling down.
Remember people living
in subways sometimes choose below over
the quote unquote attractions of this level.
Remember in outer space
a handful of overachievers
with amazing respiratory systems
manage experiments and maintenance
in the International Space Station.
I read about them
getting ready to spacewalk
hearing different songs each day
as they wake to their remoteness.
I imagine their cheeks all rosy
when they return. They're happy
but it's hard readjusting to gravity

trying to talk to their families
when they can't say exactly
how it was out there.
You should've seen it.
I wish you could've seen it, Mom.

Poem with Critical Thinking

About distant platforms—ocean ones—
and multiple scales. The subway
trumpeter playing two horns at once.
The essay I mean to write—what good is it
without radar weather, wave patterning,
permeable membrane engaged in transfer?

Standing by the sink in the morning
at the window drinking water and thinking
in this perforated way what the day
requires and what the life,
a quick blur comes into focus
off the vine garden floor.
Light brown and white framed by ice
against the blue-white of fresh powder,
scrambling from form into low
flight over the alley fence.
As if I've spoken out loud
my daughter, shivering, shoveling cereal:
"What's a critical essay?"
Loose current breaking into
Nighthawk, food chain,
sun edging over the garage.
Every surfacing relation, atmospheric
pressure, questions remaining unanswered.

The Panther

"Walking the gravel driveway
to retrieve the daily mail, a whisper surged
through the grassy field. I stopped for a long
moment—flexed, alert.
Isobars of pressure rippled my shirt
against my breasts. The world seemed
a test, as in a Borges story—the answer,
ghost, at the corner of my eye.

Once, through the front window
I watched my daughter draw sun circles
on scrap wood alongside the grain bin.
She came still, slowly tilted
her head toward the field.
I felt the call in my body
to save her, but I held.
I wanted so badly to see
what might emerge from wheat shade
into real day. Nothing. Nothing ever.

The worst of it's at night
when I wake from a dream of tangled
bodies, in love with a dead man,
to sense beyond uncertainty
the gaze upon my body.
Still, careful, I open
my eyes and find her at the bedside
whispering into dream space.
Sinuous, almost feline, she evades and I
lie alone listening through this
cloud world for breathing to surround.

Finally entirely undone
I told the man who brought our firewood:
Something watches us.
I can't trust my mind.
Out of kind curiosity, he installed cameras
like the ones he used for hunting.
I felt certain nothing visible would register.

She would be five that summer.
She and I, the survived. Alone. Alive.

When he returned with his computer
and showed the pale images
a trapdoor opened inside me.
From the blank night a shadow materialized
into a cat—square jawed and calm,
it examined the camera, crouched, circled
and came to rest on the straw mat.
The man said 'panther' and I fell
into a lower sky, strange
safety, where night was made
manifest in our depleted family.

Then he advanced the frame.
The front door opened and I knew what I would see
would change me. I would no longer suffer
ideas about love, the living or the dead.
He said the shimmer in the air
was the camera's light reflecting from her hair
but I could see he was afraid.
I mumbled something like a prayer:
protect, forgive, take me.
In the next moment everything,
even the name I had given her,
escaped me as she appeared there.

Letter Never

               Days-hours-minutes-seconds
might have fallen neatly in line with the idea.

Simplicity of following naturally multiple
momentums—perceptions came back in number
and power.
                      Easy together
with dishonest bodies.   Actions, one
into the next as far as they led. Never spiral.
Never fracture.

           Just lay out flat and wait.
Some dormant electrical pattern mistriggers,
circles inward like birds.   Light-blind
and immersive as in the channel.

I won't want to forget this and then I won't
be able to.

        One after another, they swam.

Jason Saw Sun Tunnels

for Jason Howard

When he saw photos of *Sun Tunnels*
Jason wondered if he'd recognize them
as art if he walked up. I imagined

walking up—fifty miles from anywhere
headed south along playa into water
-color sky purely blue, nearly believable.

What's gone wrong? And what slim
hope might those segments increasing
by step on the horizon represent?

For a while they're cars and the question
is whether cars exist in this time frame.
Eggs, then, gestating in one hundred

percent sun. Then clearly construction
materials on the outskirts of some invisible
development. Is the place abandoned

or invented? What kind of space suit
will the next person who sees these
lost culverts be wearing?

By now his silk shirt's drenched
and his office coif's plastered to his neck.
If the sky won't intervene

—liquidate itself and plunge the basin—
he'll die here days from freshwater.
To survive a little longer

Jason enters the tunnels for shade.
Delirium. Carved designs channel
sunlight into projections—the futile

realization that these are pieces,
commissioned, positioned
within history's weave of petroglyphs

through modern objects
in a double helix of symbolic expression
unraveled to the brink of extinction

might not come to him.
We don't know
what the walker named Jason has studied.

We think of Charlton Heston
on his knees under the ruined symbol of his nation
—it's later, Bright Eyes, not elsewhere.

Roll credits as the philosopher's body
evolves in figured light
from a nearby star.

—Nancy Holt, *Sun Tunnels*
near Lucin, Utah

Some Purple

don't forget the friend off five
weeks in silent meditation
still has a birthday
deep noticing   flies mating
in a bright kitchen   homeless veterans
distinguished victim and criminal
perched on a power line
one squirrel sings a mournful upward fifth
teach writers to feel see speak
muscular wing thrum a lilac
room conceals   shiver blown
ear to throat   emote
when relevant   evil as what
responds not to good   seven
fat ministers rear up in sexual glory
some purple   velvet celluloid
in petal folds   in eternity
                five anything
"good job of being born"

Failed Symphony

The idea of a symphony comes
as morning explosions shake new cornices
off distant ridgelines   More a feeling
organizing many sounds beautifully   Maybe a prayer
would be one part but so would explosions   Let my
friends go safely up the mountain
though light is blue and distant
rumbles launch avalanches   My friends will ski right
through the sky on burning boards to peer
through goggles at many nuclear
explosions in the sun   Just like all the stories
where God is in or behind or beyond something
my symphony will ultimately fail
to reach the future and so say God
is the future   Fraudulent
insights like God is the future the world is dead
long live the world in my symphony
linger a moment then wash away
in folk melodies like American children
vanish in tall grass so it's modern   nothing
you'd found a nation on nothing
Rimsky-Korsakov Berlioz   A giant
weather map where Wagner's low pressure
and Bach is a cold front and the Vienna
Philharmonic conducted by Wilhelm Furtwängler
heaps powder on this chalet   I'd play
my friends tumbling moguls
in bright arpeggios   The strings
laugh at the clumsy woodwinds and this window view
snow-tipped pines up the mountain   Each green needle
exhales oxygen visibly like Bruce's naked body
steaming in moonlight then diving with a quacky

little scream into snow   Also Bruce coughing up blood
Bruce altogether because despite intentions
a life can unwind before
any adequate symphony is composed

Up Kingston

"Jim Bachman's building a shack
in that canyon cutback up Kingston.
Hummingbirds live up there
it's so wet   little sparks
diving around through high grass
and sage along the melt-fed creek.
One night I suppose it was a deer
snorted at us through a thicket
and later we climbed a stone
stairway built by lord knows who or
for what purpose up the slope
toward the tree line. Before
stairs turned to faint trail through flint
shards crumbling down from the ridges
we almost stepped on a small
pale ribbon across a stone no
not a ribbon   it took a click to see
it was a creamy length of snake
lethargic on the sun remnant the rock retained.
Up top I guess a couple
of those petrified trees are gripping on
boulders now ten thousand years.
There's still a town at the bottom
where it pours out on the flat.
Truck comes every week
so he'll get his books and pills.
He's already got a regular
girl at the Bunny Ranch
but he'll need snowshoes to see her in January."

At the same time huge new planes were being built. I required

more physical activity in the postnuclear age.

I bought the land.
I'd found sands and gravels that could make concrete, clay for soil cement,
running water.

As my ideas developed I defied gravity. Without trying.
Obviously pointed at the future, all it is is

absence.

Things felt uniquely American in size and measurement.

I didn't
know much about the East and didn't like what I saw. It looked like it was
degenerating.

Fragments,
forms of evidence interest me—beautiful gravel, broken processional.

Visualize the voids combining—if you can, then you understand.

Complete the cycle—tame something wild   a rough wild rock might
fall at the base of a cliff.   Articulate that.

I had built something as big as a skyscraper. I didn't want more objects.

We found the rock water-
shot, evidence of its source directly above. The cuts are kept active. The
source   which is the enclosure becomes
false and quite arbitrary.

Physical truth in isolation
of material from source. You don't design 52-ton rocks. Size is real.
Surface work exchanges for primitive mass.

The only way out: create
objects that float.   The size of a spirit remembered in land.

It wasn't big enough. I kept working.

I decided to make the city visible

only from the inside—negative
vocabulary modulated through weather. The front wall a blast shield.

A respectable confrontation on the edge of a nuclear test site.

I wished to create the forms. I hoped to learn.

Cast off impurities. Introduce
strengthening. Propose a way of seeing. It might appear regressive
to restate volume after the negative works, but Earth potential is original,
gray.

I wondered why the voided object persisted, and where.

With such a large cut, there's an implication.

To restate
gravel under silt overburden and pile alluvial to become the mastaba.
Synthetics unobtainable due to living at the end of civilization. Wash sand
and mix it with reinforcing bar into forms. I did everything

I could with pure mass.

Anything physical becomes a statement
about absence. *Munich Depression. Nine Nevada Depressions.*

Remnants and respect accorded.

So-called unresolved
form attempts awe. Anything less finished, not killed off quite as much.
Fugitive or delicate

materials form themselves.

Inundated or eroded, extended or developed.

Feel that something

has been transcended.

In a Mountain Pasture

polluted by thinking
like the whole truth and nothing

I see slides under charged wire
one awkward calf along
river rush bound
by fire line to her
mind one heifer watching

anyway standing might be wondering
like what white nothing
washes tumbledown bother a blue
ripple ridgeline run

calves a thousand shimmers
needs I don't know
living from this stream

Poem Asleep

Native flora regain their dominance
and elephants again grow hair and tusks
upon the central grasslands of my continent.

Anxious not at all, my kept animal sleeps.

I identify the bird in the frozenberry tree
as a waxwing, not a cardinal. I struggle
—so many instances of error.

The leaves you are seeing
in the place where you live
may be beautiful, but if anything
the engine in the tissue matters.

Asleep, beauty wanders off like a Hansel.

Fresco on the concert hall ceiling
riddled with pinpoint light streams.
Fragile ribbon of oboe.
Singularity of a blue world with atmosphere.

In everything, the deepest point of the leaf
is everything. Asleep, the body is most like a leaf.

Some Parables

for Juliet Patterson

There is no special name
for the sounds old houses make
when it's twenty below, midmorning,
and the sun overtakes the pines.

There's gunfire at night
but it almost never comes closer.
It's just quiet again, though there may
be screaming elsewhere.

For the holidays, he gave the gift
of horrifying images to develop over a lifetime,
whole new continents where the fauna's
specifically evolved to devour you.

No hope is as accurate as hope.
You'll have to continue having experiences.
One thing happens and then another.
He does the awful thing every time.

Another channel in luminous flux
is as accurate as sequence that might have been
prevented. It doesn't have to determine you
or it does.

Radiant warmth, if temporary,
is practically a fact and as good a place as any
to begin. Your house is popping
in full sun, brittle cold. We could say it's alive.

Evidence Twenty

Down at the river bottom
plenty's still alive.
Evidence twenty minnows frenzied in green current
a heron feather
moist impressions
deer make in sleeping.

I've been afraid this hour of feeling
and not feeling
the newly dead with me.
I cleaned the kitchen and the bathroom
(in case they wanted to help).
Finally needing new inventory
I left the immediate
legacy of thank-yous to walk past the Ridge
Road barrier. Warm for the end
of October I crossed
a quick river on a bleaching deadfall
found a boulder in the pebble
bed of a vanished eddy
and sat near one current to contact another.

A mile away I can hear
beet trucks turn off the county road and gun it
to seventy fully loaded
on the mud-splattered highway.
People die. They make signs:
let's be safe this harvest season
and *free coffee for drivers 24/7.*
People die, I said very late one night
to Nick Plunkey and John B. Free
at Witch's Rock in the meadow under
Wheeler Peak where

John did tai chi and the galaxy
was incredibly vivid

while on our dark level
an antelope charged
and we only heard nearing
percussion in the dirt.
Isn't it unbearably sad?
They were both like, *get used to it, brother.*

Something's snapping—I don't know what—
in chin-high fronds.
A water strider attenuates this backwater.
Driving up for the queen
in this season's straight
flush of funerals
I asked my brother-in-law Mike
how many beets are in one of those giant piles of beets.
Just approximately.
Just take a guess.
But he said *who knows* meaning *who cares*
and kept flooring it. I was hoping for more
from law enforcement.

Shadow of a lady
-bug husk on the surface a little
eclipse to a bottom-feeder maybe a little
sacrament in a scramble of ceremonies.
Burn of frost on the reed stalk.
Long-winged larva on my blue pant leg.
How much? How many? Is there one
adult fish in this shallow pool
and is it a trout
because I ate pan-fried trout
fresh out of a stream once
and it was incredibly delicious

or is everything alive here
just a little baby
wing shiver fly idea
day to say goodbye.

Clip

The song had ponies in it.
The room couldn't quite bring itself to life.
The child, very young, oblivious.
Because the green curtains were half-drawn
light popped in the lens
white and occasionally kind
of ripping a bright vertical through the center.
I had this movie clip.
He's not dancing but with the music
it's like that. He sways across
and out past the edge of gray.
A car passes on the street outside.
The camera automatically un- and re-
focuses. Bare branches appear.
The house across the street
with its opaque window reflecting
our house appears. When the lens dilates
the room seems indistinct
more of a gap in space until curious
the boy reenters, now shirtless
now middle, now focus, now fore.
Soft song I liked with ponies in it
but not a child's song because the ponies
are in hell. I had this clip.
He gets closer and larger until
it's all face and a shower of hair.
A long time passes like that.
The digital image distills into dim almost
olive-colored squares. An expression
puzzle pieces of cheek and lip
corner kind of recognition breaks
like a wave from the shaky

center-eye pinpoint across as he
turns and his hand comes up and over
the lens and it ends.

Absentia

boat wake conducts evening light into many small geometries—
      all happening in an explosion—a loose phone call, a little
      bold speaking enabled by distance between people

saved in time, someone's pigtailed daughter swings above
      the hedge—sunlight prisms the image—screen between
      surfaces like lit water

the murmurs they produce, waves, degrees by the small
      combustion of the wick they light—death is a word as is life

as if more orbited than we thought satellite spins in its array—
      upswing opens downswing closes the prism, now candle on
      water, fade

I might've been Eagle Eye but for me it's a mapping drone part—
      long charts of consequence kind of marine electronica font
      ripple off as I withdraw

scrim holds original heat so it dissipates more slowly through
      weather, decades, forests, families

the brewery burn-off, certain windows kept lit after hours—the
      radiance bled through late season brush along the banks

image times thought orbits sunlight in its daughter—saved prisms
　　　fade pigtailed screen closes water

Patty says people tell story after story until the dead find a
　　　pathway

in an afterwards flush, he opens the window—"you know I'm
　　　naked"—"the world froze: I love you"

hedge daughter above image—save more—we candle someone's
　　　array downswing in lit water as if saved

a barn heaved over in grass taller than the children exiting the van
　　　in green waves

careful in thinking of my dead friend, on such a day vole tracks
　　　end at the surface brush of owl wings—"no embarrassment in
　　　being born, no glory either"

too hard the screen between closes—my boy called you *brudder*.
　　　Maybe all the sighs of this time whisper—you're napping in a
　　　side room at Christmas

more orbited than we thought—a million worlds in your blood
　　　noticed you changing—white-gold shimmer on a vapor rim—
　　　then we heard you in the kitchen—a slippery plate—a little
　　　laugh or whimper

Notes

"Channels, Currents, Crossings" was written just outside of Gimli, Manitoba, on Lake Winnipeg, and is dedicated to the Wrights: Doran, Erin, Spenser, Gavin.

"At the Edge of Perfect Adequacy" follows George Steiner's *Real Presences*.

In "Emergent," "all the time the dual working of my mind distracted me" is from Joseph Conrad's *The Secret Sharer*, and "the hopeless dream of being" is from Ingmar Bergman's *Persona*.

"Natural History" is indebted to Alvin McLane and William Fox, and to Sessions Wheeler's *Nevada's Black Rock Desert*.

Earl Madary is quoted from his Teacher of the Year Address at Viterbo University, La Crosse, Wisconsin, May 2006.

"Jason Saw Sun Tunnels" is indebted to Nancy Holt, as well as to Gerard Ferrari and Jason Howard.

"Up Kingston" is dedicated to Nick Plunkey.

"At the same time huge new planes were being built. I required more" and "I decided to make the city visible" take language from Julia Brown's interview with Michael Heizer, published in *Michael Heizer: Sculpture in Reverse* (Los Angeles: Museum of Contemporary Art, 1984), and locate it in a new context—"anything becomes a part of where it is if you take it and put it there" (Heizer).

About the Author

William Stobb is the author of five poetry collections, including the 2007 National Poetry Series selection, *Nervous Systems*. As a companion to both *Absentia* and his 2010 chapbook of desert fragments, *Artifact Eleven*, Stobb has produced an ambient voice CD, *Gone Water: Desert Dreaming*. A native of Little Falls, Minnesota, Stobb attended the University of North Dakota, where he studied poetry in the graduate writing program under the direction of the late Jay Meek. While earning a PhD at the University of Nevada, Stobb's writing was deeply influenced by the landscapes of the Great Basin, especially the Black Rock Desert, pictured on the cover of *Absentia*. With his wife and two children, Stobb lives in La Crosse, Wisconsin.

JOHN ASHBERY
Selected Poems
Self-Portrait in a Convex Mirror

TED BERRIGAN
The Sonnets

LAUREN BERRY
The Lifting Dress

JOE BONOMO
Installations

PHILIP BOOTH
Selves

JIM CARROLL
Fear of Dreaming: The
*   Selected Poems*
Living at the Movies
Void of Course

ALISON HAWTHORNE DEMING
Genius Loci
Rope

CARL DENNIS
Callings
New and Selected Poems
*   1974–2004*
Practical Gods
Ranking the Wishes
Unknown Friends

DIANE DI PRIMA
Loba

STUART DISCHELL
Backwards Days
Dig Safe

STEPHEN DOBYNS
Velocities: New and Selected
*   Poems, 1966–1992*

EDWARD DORN
Way More West: New and
*   Selected Poems*

ADAM FOULDS
The Broken Word

CARRIE FOUNTAIN
Burn Lake

AMY GERSTLER
Crown of Weeds: Poems
Dearest Creature
Ghost Girl
Medicine
Nerve Storm

EUGENE GLORIA
Drivers at the Short-Time Motel
Hoodlum Birds

DEBORA GREGER
Desert Fathers, Uranium
*   Daughters*
God
Men, Women, and Ghosts
Western Art

TERRANCE HAYES
Hip Logic
Lighthead
Wind in a Box

ROBERT HUNTER
Sentinel and Other Poems

MARY KARR
Viper Rum

WILLIAM KECKLER
Sanskrit of the Body

JACK KEROUAC
Book of Sketches
Book of Blues
Book of Haikus

JOANNA KLINK
Circadian
Raptus

JOANNE KYGER
As Ever: Selected Poems

ANN LAUTERBACH
Hum
If in Time: Selected Poems,
*   1975–2000*
On a Stair
Or to Begin Again

CORINNE LEE
PYX

PHILLIS LEVIN
May Day
Mercury

WILLIAM LOGAN
Macbeth in Venice
Strange Flesh
The Whispering Gallery

ADRIAN MATEJKA
Mixology

MICHAEL MCCLURE
Huge Dreams: San Francisco
*   and Beat Poems*

DAVID MELTZER
David's Copy: The Selected
*   Poems of David Meltzer*

ROBERT MORGAN
Terroir

CAROL MUSKE-DUKES
An Octave Above Thunder
Red Trousseau
Twin Cities

ALICE NOTLEY
Culture of One
The Descent of Alette
Disobedience
In the Pines
Mysteries of Small Houses

LAWRENCE RAAB
The History of Forgetting
Visible Signs: New and
*   Selected Poems*

BARBARA RAS
The Last Skin
One Hidden Stuff

PATTIANN ROGERS
Generations
Wayfare

WILLIAM STOBB
Absentia
Nervous Systems

TRYFON TOLIDES
An Almost Pure Empty
*   Walking*

ANNE WALDMAN
Kill or Cure
Manatee/Humanity
Structure of the World
*   Compared to a Bubble*

JAMES WELCH
Riding the Earthboy 40

PHILIP WHALEN
Overtime: Selected Poems

ROBERT WRIGLEY
Beautiful Country
Earthly Meditations: New and
*   Selected Poems*
Lives of the Animals
Reign of Snakes

MARK YAKICH
The Importance of Peeling
*   Potatoes in Ukraine*
Unrelated Individuals Forming
*   a Group Waiting to Cross*

JOHN YAU
Borrowed Love Poems
Paradiso Diaspora